GUIDEI

Children's
Ministries

*Ministries That Help
Children Grow in Faith*

Melanie C. Gordon
General Board of Discipleship

CHILDREN'S MINISTRIES

Copyright © 2012 by Cokesbury

This book is printed on acid-free paper.

ISBN 978-1-426-73643-8

Some paragraph numbers for and language in the Book of Discipline *may have changed in the 2012 revision, which was published after these Guidelines were printed. We regret any inconvenience.*

MANUFACTURED IN THE UNITED STATES OF AMERICA

Contents

Called to a Ministry of Faithfulness and Vitality

Y ou are so important to the life of the Christian church! You have consented to join with other people of faith who, through the millennia, have sustained the church by extending God's love to others. You have been called and have committed your unique passions, gifts, and abilities to a position of leadership. This Guideline will help you understand the basic elements of that ministry within your own church and within The United Methodist Church.

Leadership in Vital Ministry

Each person is called to ministry by virtue of his or her baptism, and that ministry takes place in all aspects of daily life, both in and outside of the church. Your leadership role requires that you will be a faithful participant in the **mission of the church**, which is to partner with God to **make disciples of Jesus Christ for the transformation of the world**. You will not only engage in your area of ministry, but will also work to empower others to be in ministry as well. The vitality of your church, and the Church as a whole, depends upon the faith, abilities, and actions of all who work together for the glory of God.

Clearly then, as a pastoral leader or leader among the laity, your ministry is not just a "job," but a spiritual endeavor. You are a spiritual leader now, and others will look to you for spiritual leadership. What does this mean?

All persons who follow Jesus are called to grow spiritually through the practice of various Christian habits (or "means of grace") such as prayer, Bible study, private and corporate worship, acts of service, Christian conferencing, and so on. Jesus taught his disciples practices of spiritual growth and leadership that you will model as you guide others. As members of the congregation grow through the means of grace, they will assume their own role in ministry and help others in the same way. This is the cycle of disciple making.

The Church's Vision

While there is one mission—to make disciples of Jesus Christ—the portrait of a successful mission will differ from one congregation to the next. One of your roles is to listen deeply for the guidance and call of God in your own context. In your church, neighborhood, or greater community, what are the greatest needs? How is God calling your congregation to be in a ministry of service and witness where they are? What does vital ministry look like in the life of your congregation and its neighbors? What are the characteristics, traits, and actions that identify a person as a faithful disciple in your context?

This portrait, or vision, is formed when you and the other leaders discern together how your gifts from God come together to fulfill the will of God.

Assessing Your Efforts

We are generally good at deciding what to do, but we sometimes skip the more important first question of what we want to accomplish. Knowing your task (the mission of disciple making) and knowing what results you want (the vision of your church) are the first two steps in a vital ministry. The third step is in knowing how you will assess or measure the results of what you do and who you are (and become) because of what you do. Those measures relate directly to mission and vision, and they are more than just numbers.

One of your leadership tasks will be to take a hard look, with your team, at all the things your ministry area does or plans to do. No doubt they are good and worthy activities; the question is, *"Do these activities and experiences lead people into a mature relationship with God and a life of deeper discipleship?"* That is the business of the church, and the church needs to do what only the church can do. You may need to eliminate or alter some of what you do if it does not measure up to the standard of faithful disciple making. It will be up to your ministry team to establish the specific standards against which you compare all that you do and hope to do. (This Guideline includes further help in establishing goals, strategies, and measures for this area of ministry.)

The Mission of The United Methodist Church

Each local church is unique, yet it is a part of a *connection,* a living organism of the body of Christ. Being a connectional Church means in part that all United Methodist churches are interrelated through the structure and organization of districts, conferences, and jurisdictions in the larger "family" of the denomination. *The Book of Discipline of The United Methodist Church* describes, among other things, the ministry of all United Methodist Christians, the essence of servant ministry and leadership, how to organize and accomplish that ministry, and how our connectional structure works (see especially ¶¶126–138).

Our Church extends way beyond your doorstep; it is a global Church with both local and international presence. You are not alone. The resources of the entire denomination are intended to assist you in ministry. With this help and the partnership of God and one another, the mission continues. You are an integral part of God's church and God's plan!

(For help in addition to this Guideline and the *Book of Discipline*, see "Resources" at the end of your Guideline, www.umc.org, and the other websites listed on the inside back cover.)

Guidelines in Children's Ministries

You have answered the call to serve as a minister to children. Calls come in a variety of ways, yet here you are. You may be wondering where to begin. Begin with the prayer and knowledge of the Psalmist: "O God, from my youth you have taught me / and I still proclaim your wondrous deeds. / So even to old age and grey hairs, / O God, do not forsake me, / until I proclaim your might to all the generations to come" (71:17-18).

Psalm 71 reminds us of the importance of learning and knowing the wonders of a relational God from our very beginnings. It reminds us that even as we age, our relationship with God impacts our lives today and those in future generations. The children that your ministry will touch already have a relationship with God the Father, God the Son, and God the Holy Spirit, and through your leadership it is the hope that they will grow in understanding of what God has called them to be and to do.

The Social Principles (*The Book of Discipline of The United Methodist Church*, ¶162C) state, "Once considered the property of their parents, children are now acknowledged to be full human beings in their own right, but beings to whom adults and society in general have special obligations...." This Principle calls us to take responsibility for meeting the needs of all children, not just our own, including education and protection. (See also Resolution 3081, "Child Care and the Church," in The *Book of Resolutions of The United Methodist Church*.) Whether your ministry touches three children in a small congregation, three hundred children in a large congregation, or the children who live in the community where you serve, you have been invited to gather dedicated adults and scripturally sound resources to make disciples of Jesus Christ for the transformation of the world.

Remember, you are not alone. You are in ministry with parents, guardians, grandparents, caregivers, and even ancestors who care for and about children:
- Members of the congregation who are concerned with creating and maintaining a vital church community.
- People in the community who care about the healthy development of children.
- The pastor and church leaders who are responsible for the faith development of all people.
- People within the United Methodist Connection who are here to support your ministry.
- And a story that has sustained the Christian community for thousands of years. May the Lord bless you and keep you.

A Biblical and Historical Foundation

Our first glance of Jesus is that of a newborn baby who grew and lived each phase of childhood. We may reason that Jesus experienced the love and comfort of parents and the fears, sorrows, and joys of a child. In this way, children relate to Jesus because he grew as they grow. We can assume that Jesus grew up in a home that reflected the time in which Hebrew parents were obligated to teach their children the Law and to raise them to be responsible members of the faith community. A young Jesus spoke confidently to religious authorities in the Temple, exemplifying the importance of teaching children well (Luke 2:41-52).

In ministry with children, it is important to remember that Jesus loved and honored children. Parents brought their children to be blessed by Jesus, not just in his presence, but also through his touch. Jesus publicly claimed children as models of pureness of heart and joy inherent of the kingdom of God, reminding us that we are to tend graciously to our children, and warning us of the consequences of being a "stumbling block" in our children's growth and development (see, for example, Luke 18:15-17).

Our Connectional Commitment to Children

John Wesley was also committed to the education and formation of children, and traditionally, the United Methodist Church has provided a space for children to not only learn and grow, but to be an active part of the community.

In his sermons and actions, Wesley took up the cause of children's issues, especially their intellectual and spiritual development. The Wesleyan movement inspired the development of health clinics and schools that accommodated children from all walks of life. Wesley personally visited children in workhouses and poor houses, and established Sunday schools, going against the popular writings of the time and actively participating in social justice issues that directly impacted children.

The mission of The United Methodist Church is to make disciples of Jesus Christ for the transformation of the world. This mission, which reflects Jesus' Great Commission, includes children. Faith formation for children is not an option. Leaders in ministry with children live out the Great Commission (Matthew 28:16-20) by offering opportunities, resources, and experiences for children that are steeped in the life and teachings of Jesus Christ, so this becomes your primary task.

Paragraph 256.1a of the *Book of Discipline* states that "in each local church, there shall be a church school for the purpose of accomplishing the church's educational ministry." *The Book of Resolutions,* an official document of the Church, contains three resolutions that address our commitment to children—"Putting Children and Their Families First," "Reducing the Risk of Child Sexual Abuse in the Church," and "Child Care and the Church." All leaders in ministry with children should be familiar with these documents to understand The United Methodist Church's deep commitment to children.

The general boards and agencies of The United Methodist Church take seriously the role of children in the life of the congregation. The General Board of Discipleship, through the Office of Ministry with Children, provides resources for leaders engaged in ministry with children in local congregations. The General Board of Discipleship offers a biannual *United Methodist Conference on Ministry with Children* [formerly FOCUS], and also holds the responsibility of training leaders; providing research; connecting leaders and congregations; and developing resources for use in local churches, districts, and annual conferences. The United Methodist Publishing House develops the curriculum component for children, and a Curriculum Resources Committee reviews curriculum for alignment with United Methodist theology.

The General Board of Global Ministries advocates for children worldwide and supports United Methodist Women in the *Campaign for Children,* which focuses on advocating for greater support for public schools in the United States. The General Board of Church and Society advocates for children in legislative issues. The Commission on United Methodist Men supports the office of Civic Youth Agencies/Scouting. The General Commission on Finance and Administration provides support for congregations in matters of risk and in keeping children safe.

Most annual conferences have a children's council and a person responsible for children's ministries. There are also people within each district who are knowledgeable about district and annual conference programs and support for those who work with children. Christian Educators Fellowship will share their knowledge and skills in ministry with children.

God loves all children and desires relationship with all children, and as Christians we are called to cultivate that relationship. John Wesley desired for children to know and love God. Our heritage as United Methodists has shown a commitment to children through baptism, Sunday school, Bethlehem Centers, daycare centers for working parents, and homes for children. The United Methodist Church continues to name children as vital participants in the community whom God calls us to love, protect, and nurture.

Your Role as a Spiritual Leader

You are a vital part of the Connection, and how you live out your life in accord with the biblical and historical principles of the Church will have a direct impact on children and their families. In Paul's letter to the community at Ephesus, he appealed to his sisters and brothers to live into the unity of Spirit that God desires of us through Jesus Christ—One body, one Spirit, one Lord, one faith, one baptism (Ephesians 4:1-7). Those called in children's ministry live into this unity, and they use their gifts to serve the children of the congregation and the larger community in a multitude of ways. It is important to remember that God has given each of us gifts to be used to build up the community of faith (4:11-13).

As a leader in The United Methodist Church, you set the example for the people that you lead—the children. Your life both publically and privately should reflect the life and teachings of Jesus Christ. It is difficult to teach that which we do not practice or understand. The General Rules (*Discipline*, ¶104) set forth a rule of life to aid in that practice. Marjorie Thompson, in *Soul Feast*, tells us that "a *rule of life* is a pattern of spiritual disciplines that provides structure and direction for growth in holiness. . . . It fosters gifts of the Spirit in personal life and human community, helping to form us into the persons God intends us to be" (p. 138, italics added). The General Rules expect us to begin by doing no harm and doing good, then to attend upon the ordinances of God by loving God through regular practice of the public worship of God; the ministry of the Word, either read or expounded; the Supper of the Lord; family and private prayer; searching the Scriptures; and fasting or abstinence.

While they are not specifically mentioned in this section of the *Discipline*, Wesley would include works of advocacy, service, and justice among them. All these practices will direct your life and support your ministry "to witness to Jesus Christ in the world, and to follow his teachings through acts of compassion, justice, worship, and devotion under the guidance of the Holy Spirit" (*Discipline*, ¶1117.2).

Self-care is your gift to God, those you serve, and to you. Jesus visited Mary, Martha, and Lazarus when he needed to take respite. It is important to follow this model. Plan wisely. Set boundaries. Take time to care for yourself. Taking time for renewal is a discipline that will allow you to grow in holiness.

Ministry with Children

a vital, disciple-making congregation provides multiple opportunities for children to participate in the life of the church. "As people of faith, we are called to teach children through scripture, our tradition as Methodists, the Social Principles, the ritual of baptism, and our concern for families. In responding to the call set before us, we will provide environments for children to be nurtured in the faith and to grow as children of God" ("Child Care and the Church," #3081, *Book of Resolutions*).

The Spiritual Lives of Children

Children are spiritual beings born with the essential knowledge of God's presence, and with the potential for spiritual experiences with God to activate that potential. The role of those who are responsible for their faith development is to help children on their spiritual journey. Scripture gives the example of Jesus growing strong and gaining in wisdom in his community (Luke 2:40). A congregation that intentionally fulfills this role actively:
- creates experiences that support children in the knowledge and awareness of God
- models God's unconditional love for all of God's children
- provides opportunities that support children in discovering, developing, and sharing their unique gifts from God
- listens and responds to the needs of children

SMALL GROUPS AND COVENANT

Making disciples of Jesus Christ for the transformation of the world in a vital congregation includes multiple opportunities for children to participate in small groups. Small groups include all ministries within children's ministry that include a smaller group of children. These are opportunities for children to form deeper relationships with each other and with God. Helping children develop a covenant for each of these groups will equip them to recognize the importance of covenant as is found in Scripture and in our Wesleyan heritage.

The Digital Child in Christian Community

The children whom we serve today are born surrounded by more technological advances than many of us could have ever imagined. Depending on your setting, you will encounter children who are savvy with technology from as early as eighteen months old to children whose families do not have the resources to offer them handheld technology. Most of them will fall somewhere in between. Your role in children's ministry is to understand how children learn in light of the digital age, and to recognize the importance of forming relationship in community where all of the senses are engaged. Technology lacks the ability of the human touch. Technology cannot give safe hugs. Technology cannot console the grief-stricken child. It is a tool that can connect us to one another in new ways that can be healthy and encouraging.

In Jesus' childhood, we can assume that he grew up in a culture where children were formed and educated through relationships and face-to-face communication. Your primary formational tools are communication and building relationship. Help children actively build relationships with peers, family members, and in the gathered community of Christ using these media only to enhance those relationships.

Getting Started

a s coordinator of children's ministries, you are "responsible for assuring that children are considered and included within the life of the congregation. The coordinator will lead the children's council, when organized, and will work closely with clergy and other program-related staff. The coordinator will vision, plan, and advocate for children, particularly in the areas of faith development, safety, and discipleship. The coordinator will work with other leaders in the congregation to assure that policies and procedures are in place to help keep all children and the adults who care for and work with them safe." These policies and procedures include such things as background checks, having at least two adults per group, and cardiopulmonary resuscitation and first-aid training. "The coordinator will also advocate for mission education for children, including The United Methodist Children's Fund for Christian Mission" (*Discipline*, ¶ 256.2a).

Each District Office and each Annual Conference office has access to the *District Training Model for Ministry with Children* developed by Ministry with Children of the General Board of Discipleship. This comes in print and media versions for use in New Church Starts, Self-Study, and a Group Retreat. Look for it at www.gbod.org/children.

Your Ministry as a Children's Leader

In most congregations that serve a small number of children each week, the coordinator of children's ministry is probably the primary person responsible for seeing that the needs of children are met. In most large membership congregations who serve a large number of children, the coordinator of children's ministry may be one of several age-level coordinators. Medium membership congregations serve various numbers of children, so the children's ministry may be served by a coordinator and/or by a children's minister on the church staff.

If your congregation employs a staff person responsible for children's ministry, your job may be modified in relation to the staff person's duties and whether that person is employed full- or part-time. Although the responsibilities of your role as coordinator of children's ministries may vary, your primary task remains the faithful formation of children as they journey as disciples of Jesus Christ. Depending on the size and staffing of your church, your responsibilities may include these practices and tasks.

Always begin with prayer. This is the one means of grace that we can practice alone and in community and the one that is God's gift of communication with God. Pray intentionally for the children and their families.

Gather information that will guide your ministry with children by talking with key individuals and groups in the congregation, exploring the resources that you have in your local church, and contacting the General Board of Discipleship and your Annual Conference for support and resources.

Create a plan of communication with parents, guardians, and teachers of the children in your congregation.

Know the children. Learn the name of each child that you will serve in children's ministry. Address the children by name. Always know how many children you serve. Each child is a gift from God and deserves to be remembered and counted.

Suggest and seek experiences that may be new or innovative in children's ministries.

Advocate. Identify key people in the congregation and community who are advocates for children's needs and issues. Advocate that all children are welcome and expected to participate in the full life of the church as vital participants. Advocate for quality leadership. Stay informed on the gifts of church members. Advocate for sufficient funding. Keep the financial planners aware of the needs of all ministries with children.

Set realistic and innovative goals. Appropriate goals are measurable, have a reasonable timetable for accomplishment, and fit the vision.

Assure training opportunities for teachers and leaders.

Be safe. Adopt a Safe Sanctuaries® policy and enforce it so that the congregation is a safe place for children and for the adults who engage with them. Know the Safe Sanctuaries® policy in your annual conference. The contact list for Safe Sanctuaries® is on the Children's Ministry website of the General Board of Discipleship. (See also Resources.)

Use approved resources. Acquaint yourself with the curriculum and resource materials available from The United Methodist Publishing House through Cokesbury. Look for approved curriculum with the Curriculum Resources Committee logo [CRC].

Stay connected and communicate. Partner with leaders in the congregation who work with youth, adults, and families. As children grow, the transition to youth ministries will run more smoothly if you plan intergenerational activities. Communicate with leaders of groups with whom children's ministries share space, such as the Girl Scouts, Boy Scouts, or Alcoholics Anonymous. Open communication will allow everyone to work well in community. Connect with leaders in ministry with children at other United Methodist churches, as well as with other denominations and non-profits. A network of people who care for children is a valuable resource.

Building Relationships

Building relationships with ministry leaders and other stakeholders is crucial to creating a vital community for making disciples. Your responsibility with children places you in a unique position to serve on various committees of the church and to enter into relationships with children's family members.

See the Collaboration Cycle graphic on the Guidelines CD.

RELATIONSHIPS WITH OTHER MINISTRY LEADERS

Talk with the pastor or staff person with whom you relate to establish expectations of your involvement with committees and other ministries of the church. Someone should represent concerns of children as events are planned and decisions are made. Advocate for the inclusion of children's needs. Church size does not matter. Even in a very small congregation, it is important to have an advocate for children. Recruit others who care about children to act as advocates as decisions are made.

Although children's ministry relates to various groups within the church structure, there are those that have a direct impact on children's ministry. Advocate serving on these various committees and councils to see to the spiritual needs of the children in the congregation and the community.

Church Council provides for planning and implementing a ministry of nurture, outreach, witness, and resources; and serves as the administrative agency of the charge conference in the local church.

Nurture Ministry in the local church encompasses education, Christian formation, and small groups (at least). All of these areas directly impact the work of children's ministry. In addition, the witness and outreach ministries are important places to include a voice for the needs of children and as an outlet for teaching them about service.

The Council on Children's Ministries is responsible for planning, implementing, executing, and evaluating children's ministry in the local church. Although this group is led by the coordinator of children's ministries, this may vary depending on the size of the church. If the coordinator of children's ministries leads this group, it is important to invite individuals who share the same characteristics of those in all effective leadership ministries. The council on children's ministries "shall be responsible for planning, visioning, and advocating for children within the congregation, the community, and the world. The council will set policies and procedures related to children, oversee the planning of short-term experiences, consider children's ministry needs within the whole of the congregation's ministries, and communicate with parents and the congregation. The children's council will work closely with the coordinator of children's ministries and church staff responsible for ministry with children, including children's choirs and weekday ministries. The children's council is accountable to the group responsible for the local church's educational ministry" (*Discipline*, ¶ 256.2b).

A Weekday Ministries Advisory Board is responsible to the church and the weekday preschool ministry to assure that policies, budget, personnel, space, and program regulations are implemented and adhered to by the director of the weekday preschool. "The term *weekday ministry* applies to any regularly planned ministry for children. When appropriate, one or more weekday ministry boards may be organized to oversee the weekday ministry programs of the congregation. The board's membership should be mostly professing members of the congregation, with parent, church staff, and weekday ministry staff representatives. The board will set policies consistent with the congregation's policies, state mandates, and sound business practices. The board will guide weekday ministries as appropriate opportunities for faith development, mission outreach, Christian education, evangelism, and safety. They will advocate for inclusion of children from various socioeconomic, cultural, and racial/ethnic backgrounds. Weekday ministry board(s) accountability should be placed within the local church organizational structure with consideration to the group responsible for the congregation's education ministry" [¶ 256.2c].

RELATIONSHIPS WITH CHILDREN AND FAMILIES

In Luke 2, Jesus talked with the religious teachers in the Temple as his parents searched for him. Although Jesus was in his Father's house, his parents fretted over not knowing where their child was. We want children to feel that the church is their Safe Sanctuary, and we want to assure parents and guardians that their children are in a safe and nurturing community. Building relationships with children and their families is the first step in creating a vital children's ministry. It is important to:

- Listen to children and take an interest in their lives. They live in a world where they are very rarely listened to.
- Address all children by name. This creates intimacy and makes children feel special.
- Communicate with parents and guardians frequently and regularly. Use all of the tools available to connect with parents.
- Include parents and guardians in evaluation of the children's ministry. They observe in ways that are important to children's ministry.
- Know the parents and address them by name. This sounds daunting if you are in a large church, but calling a parent by name helps parents to know that they are considered a part of the community. This will also make the parents and guardians more comfortable sharing their comments and concerns as they relate to their children.

Creating an Effective Ministry Group

The ritual of the baptismal covenant of The United Methodist Church retells the story of the importance of covenant in our journey as disciples of Christ. Developing a covenant with the ministry group will not only honor this tradition, but will help you to encourage one another while holding each other accountable in a way that gives an "account of what you have done and not done to build up the body of Christ and to grow in holiness of heart and life." Each member has input and a voice in the building and keeping of the covenant. When building a covenant, consider everyone's ideas. You may want to offer the following as a starting point. Sample Covenants can be found on the General Board of Discipleship website under *Covenant Discipleship*.

- We will balance the time we devote to school, church, work, family, and friends, including our own spiritual and recreational life.
- We will spend some time each day in prayer for the children of this congregation and the world.
- We will practice listening to other people as a ministry of grace.
- We will not be silent when confronted with social injustice, and we will witness for justice, inclusiveness, and equality and will encourage reconciliation wherever possible.
- We will be faithful in attendance and participation in worship each Sunday.
- We will pray for those who lead us in worship each week, and especially for the pastor.
- We will speak to one another with respect.

Effective teachers and leaders communicate well, build healthy working relationships, continue to improve their skills, and advocate for what they believe in. Although this skill set looks like someone who is extroverted and assertive, these skills are present in all people who lead groups well. The role of those in children's ministry is to tap into the gifts of the people in the congregation and community, provide opportunities for them to share these gifts with the children in your ministry, and offer opportunities for these skills to develop.

IDENTIFYING TEACHERS AND LEADERS

As you look around for people to share in this ministry, start with basics. Make a list of people who attend worship often and regularly, pray, read and study the Bible, give time and money to support the ministries of the church, and have a genuine concern about a sound faith formation of children. Go deeper in discovering the potential for leaders and teachers by looking at the following gifts and commitments:

Passion: People who demonstrate a deep commitment to the faithful formation of children and advocate for the needs of children.

Character: People who demonstrate and model a mature Christian faith and who practice the means of grace frequently and regularly.

Knowledge of Ministry: People who possess appropriate experience and/or academic credentials in Christian education; share knowledge of the Bible and biblical interpretation; demonstrate a basic knowledge of child development; and are familiar with United Methodist history, doctrine, polity, and tradition.

Professional Practices: People who are committed to quality in all areas of ministry, understand the importance of undergoing a background check and other Safe Sanctuaries® requirements, will take direction, are equipped to lead, exhibit positive interpersonal skills, and will participate in ongoing training.

TRAINING OPPORTUNITIES

Even the most experienced teachers and leaders in children's ministry will benefit from training and enrichment events to keep them fresh and to support one another. Plan for some combination of these opportunities.
* Plan a yearly retreat that combines training, information, and fun.
* Ask a church or community member with a specific expertise to share some ideas with the children's ministry group.
* Invite a local teacher to lead a workshop on classroom management. An experienced teacher will offer tips on addressing issues that come up frequently.

- Contact the district office, annual conference office, and the General Board of Discipleship for free and low-cost audio/visual training. This will alleviate the cost of paying a speaker each time training is needed.
- Connect with other United Methodist churches to plan joint training events for teachers and leaders. All congregations are concerned with faithful formation of children.

COMMUNICATING WITH TEACHERS AND LEADERS

Face-to-face communication is vital to building strong leadership in children's ministry. Scripture exemplifies the importance of person-to-person contact. The current reality is that we communicate more and more through technology, which is a wonderful tool when used wisely. As technology evolves, evolve with it. Use it to send updates, check on meeting dates, and issue reminders and announcements. But, your primary mode of communication must be in person where you will gain a deeper understanding of individuals by tone of voice, facial expression, and human touch. Plan regular meetings that give teachers and leaders an opportunity to voice opinions, compare notes on activities, evaluate past events, and support one another through covenant.

Planning for Children's Ministry

the liturgical calendar defines the seasons and holy days of the Christian year. It stands as an example of the importance of preparation. A well-planned calendar places you in a proactive position, and can minimize conflicts with events taking place in the local and general church, and in your community. Your children and families can plan well in advance so that they can more freely participate in activities. As you plan, keep in mind the essential process of starting with your intentional goals, then plan for how you will meet those goals so that you reach out to children, nurture them, equip them for discipleship, and then send them out (in age-appropriate ways) as disciples.

A Calendar for Ministry with Children

This calendar is a basic place for you to begin in your ministry context. As you plan your calendar, include dates for meetings, financial reconciliations, programs, community activities, paperwork due dates, training, deadlines, and publicity. *The Official United Methodist Program Calendar,* available through United Methodist Communications, is a valuable planning tool, which includes the special dates and observances and prompts you in earlier months to begin planning. Some of the items here will help you to work and plan ahead and others indicate the time something is happening.

JANUARY
- Covenant with a small group to serve as leaders in ministry with children in your congregation.
- Gather your children's ministry group to work on the ministries and programs through the church year, starting with Advent (four Sundays before Christmas, often starting the last Sunday in November). Beginning with Advent gives you the opportunity to set your calendar eleven months in advance. In larger churches, you may want to allow for more advanced planning.
- Celebrate Human Relations Day.
- Offer a training opportunity for children's leaders.
- Plan for a Lenten study for children.

FEBRUARY
- Celebrate African American History Month.
- Plan for vacation Bible school for children of all ages (and collaborate with other age level leaders, if VBS is intergenerational).
- Offer a gesture of appreciation to children's teachers and leaders.

MARCH

- Partner with the family ministries leader to observe Christian Home month in May.
- Plan for Peace with Justice Sunday.
- Celebrate World Day of Prayer.

APRIL

- Celebrate Earth Day.
- Celebrate One Great Hour of Sharing (the fourth Sunday in Lent).
- Offer an intergenerational day of service in the community.
- Evaluate children's ministry: participation, children's needs and concerns, feedback from parents, feedback from leadership.

MAY

- Celebrate Christian Home Month.
- Celebrate Older Adult Recognition Day.
- Celebrate Aldersgate Day.
- Organize teacher training opportunities for fall.
- Offer a gesture of appreciation for all leaders of children.
- Invite children to give feedback on what they experienced in children's ministry activities.
- Create and distribute a list of activities to keep children and families connected during the summer months.
- Distribute and review program evaluations to leaders, parents, and guardians.

JUNE

- Offer a training opportunity for children's leaders.
- Review and update curriculum and resources.

JULY

- Participate in United Methodist training opportunities, like The United Methodist Conference on Children [formerly FOCUS].
- Review the covenant that children's teachers and leaders have made with one another.
- Prepare for charge conference.

AUGUST

- Provide a back-to-school blessing and celebration for children and their families.
- Celebrate Promotion Sunday.
- Download the planning manual for Children's Sabbath, and organize a weekend of service activities.
- Plan for Advent.

SEPTEMBER
- Celebrate Hispanic Heritage Month.
- Offer a Communion study for families with children.

OCTOBER
- Celebrate Children's Sabbath.
- Celebrate World Communion Sunday.
- Organize teacher training opportunities for spring.

NOVEMBER
- Celebrate All Saints Day.
- Distribute a prayer calendar for Advent.
- Offer a Parents' Night Out.

DECEMBER
- Celebrate the birth of our Lord, Jesus Christ.

Creating a Budget

The issue of money was addressed repeatedly by Jesus. In order to live into our Christian identity, it is important to use our resources well. Some congregations will have ample budgets for children's ministry, while others may struggle with a tiny budget. One important thing to remember is that you are the advocate for faith formation of children, and the congregation should invest in the children of the church and community. You may be asked by the finance committee to make recommendations about the budget for children's ministry as they plan for a new fiscal year. Having this information on hand will greatly assist that process and help them create a realistic budget. Fiscal responsibility is part of your role as a leader in children's ministry, so keep these things in mind each year:

- Consider what experiences you want to offer for children
- Develop a budget and justify each line item
- Perform a monthly reconciliation of the budget to actual costs
- Calculate the average cost per child per year
- Calculate the cost per age group, identifying the most and least costly
- Ask for what you need and be aware of what teachers or others pay for themselves

Training Opportunities

Build in at least one training retreat for the year. This may be a district training, an annual conference event on children's issues, or a national Children's Ministry conference offered by the General Board of Discipleship. This time serves three purposes. It gives teachers, leaders, and volunteers the opportunity to more deeply understand the work to which they are called, an opportunity to connect with those in other ministry settings who work with children, and an opportunity to build relationship with those with whom they work. It is important to stay updated on children's issues as children are exposed to more information more rapidly each year. Consider the following:

- First Aid and CPR
- Safe Sanctuaries®
- Helping children deal with grief
- Brain development of children
- Faith development of children
- Positive discipline
- Spiritual lives of children
- Addressing bullying
- Storytelling
- Building intergenerational relationships
- Helping children build covenant disciple groups
- Self care for the teacher
- Including children with special needs
- Helping children through transitions

Selecting Resources and Curriculum

As the proverb goes, "Train children in the right way, and when old, they will not stray" (Proverbs 22:6). Selecting developmentally appropriate curriculum and resources is a daunting task, but one that must be taken seriously. The traditional models of teaching catered to a specific kind of learner, and other children had to adapt. We know that children learn differently, and at different rates, so it is reasonable to explore options that offer experiences for the whole child.

We are fortunate that research has given us a better perspective of development than any previous generation. We know that the days of sitting at a table with a Sunday school book that has a story followed by questions and a Scripture to memorize only allow the very minimal opportunity to experience God. We know that children learn differently and learn through experience. We know that children learn best in secure surroundings. We know that milestones in the lives of children should be acknowledged and celebrated.

In the process of selecting curriculum and resources, care must be taken in the way that Scripture is interpreted for our children. Many curricula that are available are not aligned with the United Methodist doctrine of grace and should be considered appropriately. The Curriculum and Resource Selection Checklist (on the CD) can assist you in choosing curriculum that allows children to deepen their experience of God the Father, Son, and Holy Spirit, in a way that stays true to our United Methodist heritage.

Evaluation of Children's Ministry

Each year, it is important to evaluate the children's ministries in your congregation. Open evaluations to the children's ministry leadership group, other ministry leaders, parents, and children.

Several evaluation or planning checklists and visual planning helps are on the Guidelines CD or at www.gbod.org/children:
• Children as Vital Participants in the Life of the Congregation
• Evaluation Cycle (graphic)
• Collaboration Cycle for Planning (graphic)
• Curriculum and Resource Selection Checklist
• Evaluation of Children's Ministry
• Parent Evaluation of Children's Ministry
• Checklist for Implementing and Maintaining the Basics of Safe Sanctuaries®

The *Evaluation Cycle* graphic depicts a process for developing strategies that begins with identifying the specific, intentional results you want to achieve through your children's ministry. Then, within the several stages of the discipling cycle (reach out, nurture, equip, and send), you set your strategies for how you will work with children of all ages to promote their growth through those stages. But how do you know if you are accomplishing what you want?

Attendance or other "countable" indicators are helpful. Those *quantifiable* attainments are easy to recognize: 40 new children in the Sunday school, 5 percent growth in participation in VBS, and so on. For each of the strategies, establish your target measures for what will be considered a "success," and be sure not to confuse measures with strategies. These measures must be age-appropriate and describe what will have happened, not just what you do and how you do it, but the outcome for the people who do it. If, for example, the desired result is "knowing and practicing the spiritual disciplines" one strategy for early readers might be to provide written copies of the Lord's Prayer and to say it together weekly in each class or group. A specific activity for that strategy might be for children to decorate their prayer as a colorful mini-poster. The *quantifiable* measures relate, for example, to how many children made the poster, how many weeks they recited it, how many learned it by heart, and so on.

While you want to see good numbers and increased percentages, they do not tell the entire story. In addition, looking only at what is happening with children and not the adults who work with the children omits an important set of measures. Children have a profound ability to teach adults lessons in generosity, humility, cooperation, simplicity, inclusiveness, and love. Those intangible measures (or perhaps you use the term *metrics*) are the *qualitative* indicators of whether a life is being formed and transformed in the image of God, which is the ultimate goal.

To continue the "Lord's Prayer" example, the *qualitative* measures relate to how well the children understand it, how they have learned about God from it, and what it means to them—in age-appropriate ways. (For in-depth help in setting measures and doing evaluation, see also the *Measures Evaluation Tool* and other helps in the "Setting Goals" tab at www. umvitalcongregations.org.)

You may be asked to report, or to provide information for a staff member's report, to comply with the annual conference requirements for data related to the conference's strategic growth goals. To this end, you will want to track and record the number of participants, including the trend (up or down) in that attendance, in all the functions, classes, groups, and experiences planned for ministry with children. In addition to the number of children, you will also want to note the number of adult (and youth) volunteers who help to provide for this ministry.

Equally important, be intentional about collecting the stories that children, teachers, and group leaders share about what is happening to them as a result of their efforts and participation. It is in these narratives, either self-reported or witnessed by others, that you can see the changes in faith maturity, life choices, acquired spiritual disciplines, and other fruits of the Spirit.

Sharing Space

Sharing space in a church building can be challenging. The doors of our churches should always remain open to the community and the ministries of the church. As a leader in the church, your role is to create an atmosphere where ministries and programs can live together in the space allowed. These suggestions from *Sharing Space,* an article by Melanie C. Gordon, will be helpful as you address the needs of space in your setting.

- Continually look at ways to improve communication and relationship between the church education staff, the weekday ministries staff, and the leaders of groups that meet in the areas designated for children's ministry.
- Develop and maintain mechanisms to bring people to the table to work through issues constructively regarding use of space.

- Develop policies that allow ongoing communication concerning issues around space between the weekday ministries and church committees.
- Communicate with one another so that there is more of a focus on community rather than individuality.
- Develop a budget process to maintain ongoing ministries adequately, given varying economic climates.
- Set an example for children through your actions and decisions on shared space.

Creating Safe Sanctuaries®

Whoever welcomes one such child in my name welcomes me. If any of you put a stumbling block before one of these little ones who believe in me, it would be better for you if a great millstone were fastened around your neck and you were drowned in the depth of the sea. Woe to the world because of stumbling blocks! Occasions for stumbling are bound to come, but woe to the one by whom the stumbling block comes!" (Matthew 18:6-9).

It is unfortunate that the children whom God places in our care can and have become victims of sexual abuse in the very place where they should feel safe—the church. It is your responsibility as a leader in children's ministry to work with others in leadership and ministry with children to create a safe space for children to grow in love of God and neighbor. Therefore, as *Safe Sanctuaries* points out, each church *must* have updated policies, procedures, and insurance coverage to protect children and those engaged in ministry with children. This is not optional. (See the Guidelines CD for sample forms and check lists, or use the ones that are in *Safe Sanctuaries*.)

The Social Principles of The United Methodist Church state that "children must be protected from economical, physical, emotional and sexual abuse and exploitation and abuse" (¶162C), and the 1996 General Conference of The United Methodist Church adopted Resolution 3084, *Reducing the Risk of Child Sexual Abuse in the Church*. That Resolution notes, "Most annual conferences can cite specific incidents of child sexual abuse and exploitation within churches. Virtually every congregation has among its members adult survivors of early sexual trauma. Such incidents are devastating to all who are involved: the child, the family, the local church, and its leaders. Increasingly, churches are torn apart by the legal, emotional, and monetary consequences of litigation following allegations of abuse." It is imperative that this be taken seriously.

- Require every person working directly with children to undergo a background check.
- Require every person working directly with children to participate in Safe Sanctuaries® training annually.
- Educate the congregation.
- Educate the parents.
- Educate the children.
- Include an accountability statement in the covenant to adhere to Safe Sanctuaries® standards.
- Stay current on developments in Safe Sanctuaries® by contacting your Annual Conference or the General Board of Discipleship.

Addressing Special Needs

J esus shared a special connection with people who lived with disabilities, exemplifying for us that all children are welcome participants in the life of the church. It is the responsibility of the leaders in ministry with children to advocate for the accommodation and participation of children who live with disabilities, working with the trustees and others in leadership.

A welcoming congregation makes sure that architecture allows individuals with physical disabilities to navigate the space. Attitudes are based in a community's knowledge and understandings about disabilities. Good communication includes the use of sight and sound that allow the least restrictive opportunity for participation. Programs allow individuals with disabilities an opportunity to share their gifts and talents with the community. Liturgical practices, such as sacraments or rituals, are adapted to meet individual needs.

Other basic needs for children with disabilities:
- Provide appropriate support for families of children with disabilities.
- Design ministries that include children with disabilities.
- Prepare and train teachers to address the needs of children with disabilities.
- Teach the congregation to use inclusive language. Do not use the word *handicapped* and avoid phrases like "the deaf kid"; rather use the word *disabled*, and refer to children as "John, who has autism."
- Include children with disabilities in all child-appropriate activities in the life of the church.
- Learn about and provide adapted materials for reading, drawing, coloring, or painting.
- Allow for use of multiple intelligences.
- Make audio books and books on computer available.
- Provide adapted utensils to self-feed.
- Provide adapted brushes, pencils, and markers that are easier to grip.
- Pre-cut items and put glue down while the child pastes them by pressing them down.
- Tape papers to table so they will not move around when trying to paint, draw, or color.
- Use instruments that can be strapped to the body or hand.
- Use seating that allows children to be on similar levels.

Ministry in the Community and the World

the Great Commission tells us first to "go" and make disciples, and John Wesley did just that. Children's ministry goes beyond the walls of the church. Wesley used his financial resources to buy food for poor families, hire a teacher for children in the school, and purchase wool for children in workhouses. Wesley also visited children in workhouses, orphanages, and poorhouses to witness and advocate for justice for children. Today, we may live out this scriptural and historical heritage through mission, evangelism and witness, stewardship, and advocacy as we care for children.

Mission

It is important that children participate in mission opportunities locally and globally. Jesus preached about the importance of serving the poor, and John Wesley's ministry for children had a running theme of serving children who would otherwise go without. Some of these children may be in your congregation, and they are certainly in the community and in the world. Collaborate with community organizations and other faith communities to find out the needs of the children in your community, and then ask the children in your children's ministry to imagine ways to serve those children.

On the global level, participate in The United Methodist Children's Fund for Christian Mission. This is a joint ministry of the General Board of Discipleship and the General Board of Global Ministries that undertakes projects in which children learn more about children around the world and about the practice of mission. These resources are available for free download through the GBOD Children's Ministry website.

Additional opportunities that allow children to be actively involved with mission are through UMCOR, the United Methodist Committee on Relief. UMCOR provides relief following disasters in the United States and worldwide through relief kits that can be built at the local church level. Also consider supporting UNICEF, Heifer Project International, ZOE Ministries, and CROP walks. All of these organizations offer child-friendly resources and mission opportunities for children.

Annual conferences, the United Methodist Women, and districts also offer opportunities to live into our call to social justice. In all mission opportunities, make sure that children understand that this is an opportunity to serve and to learn from others.

Evangelism and Witness

One important way to make disciples is through inviting children from the community to participate in the ministries and programs of the church. Opportunities for evangelism can be intentional or serendipitous, but always be prepared.

Your congregation can evangelize children and families through offering ministries that support families in a nurturing, safe, and Christ-like environment. Evaluate the needs of your community in the areas of after-school care, tutoring, daycare, ill-child care, and hunger. Look at the gifts of your congregation to discern how you can meet these and other needs.

Talk to the children about their faith story. Ask them regularly and often their thoughts on God, Jesus, the Church, love, and doing good. Knowing how to articulate what they believe will give them the tools that they need to talk about their faith to others and to connect what they believe with who they are in the world.

Stewardship

Jesus talked about stewardship nearly as much as he talked about the kingdom of God. Teaching children to use God's gifts wisely is important to care for the Creation and giving to the church. Stewardship goes beyond monetary giving. Stewardship encompasses care for Creation, service to God and others, sharing our gifts, participation in worship, and understanding sacrifice.

Talk to children about the work of the church, including missions, Creation care, advocacy, and evangelism. Provide opportunities for them to see how the money that they place in the offering plate supports the work of the church.

Advocacy

Through words and action, John Wesley advocated for poor children through providing education for all, visiting families, establishing health clinics, and giving as important to Christian life. As a leader in children's ministry, it is your role to advocate for children within the church and in the world. It is also your role to share with the congregation the importance of this ministry. The General Board of Church and Society advocates on behalf of the rights of children "by working toward the elimination of all forms of discrimination and oppression of children and by affirming positive initiatives that result in an enhancement of the quality of life for children."

The Children's Defense Fund coordinates resources and materials for Children's Sabbath each year. This interreligious event is the opportunity for the church to bring children's issues to the attention of the community through activities, mission, and worship. A guide to Children's Sabbath is available for free download through GBOD or The Children's Defense Fund each August for this October observance.

Inclusiveness and Ecumenical Awareness

When the Great Commission calls us to make disciples, it adds, "of all nations." We are to go out into the world—a world filled with people who differ from us physically, socioeconomically, culturally, and educationally. This commission is not limited to those who are in our country or look like us or speak the same language or celebrate like we do. There are many opportunities for children to learn about others who are different from themselves—whether it is in terms of race, ethnicity, economics, physical or mental ability, or religious beliefs.

- Be intentional in providing opportunities for children to learn about and to appreciate others.
- Provide anti-bias training for adults who work with children.
- Provide opportunities for learning about other faith communities.
- Invite teachers and children from other faith communities to share their traditions and beliefs.
- Observe Children's Sabbath with people from other faith communities.
- Collaborate with other congregations for Vacation Bible School.

Ministries Related to Children's Ministries

Children's ministry does not stand alone in the formation of children, but with a variety of ministries dedicated to making disciples of Jesus Christ. It is important to work together so that all children can know the breadth and depth of what it means to be a disciple for life.

CAMPING MINISTRIES

Every annual conference provides a variety of camping opportunities for children. Camping ministry invites children to seek God and to grow spiritually. This is an opportunity for Christian love in action. Children have the opportunity to become friends through living together, sharing the responsibilities of community embarking on new adventures, and reflecting on the meaning of life. All of this occurs in the midst of nature, which can greatly enhance the awareness of and love for God. The lessons learned can be applied to inspire and lead others when children return to their communities of faith and society at large. The camp experience serves as a reminder for children and leaders that we are all God's representatives meant to care for the whole community of Creation—people and the natural world.

YOUTH MINISTRIES

Youth ministry is the next step for the children in your congregation. This ministry seeks to form relationships and connections for youth, giving them the opportunity to feel a part of something bigger than themselves. Youth are challenged to develop a healthy and authentic relationship with God, peers, and adults through worship, activities, study, and mission opportunities. At this stage, it is the opportunity for young people to lead while being trained and equipped for leadership. Like children's ministry, youth ministry includes the entire family.

FAMILY MINISTRIES

Family ministry is identifying and enabling all to see Christ-like relationship qualities among those who call each other family, equipping households to be centers of faith, providing to those households of faith opportunities for mission and service, and attracting others to be part of the congregation. All children belong to God's family and to a group of people they call family. Family ministry deeply impacts the process of making disciples as the children's ministry goes beyond the church and community into the home.

SCOUTING MINISTRIES

Boy Scouts of America, Girl Scouts of the USA, Big Brothers Big Sisters (Amachi Partnership), Camp Fire USA, and 4-H offer opportunities to minister to young people. They each encompass Christian teachings and a long-standing connection with local congregations. The Church is endowed with certain responsibilities that allow scouting and civic youth serving programs to become a ministry, and this differentiates scouting ministries from a civic or community-based club.

Weekday Ministries

John Wesley set the example for us as Methodists as he began health clinics and schools for the children to learn to read and encouraged the pastors to meet with the children regularly. His call to meet the needs of people where they were stands as a marker for us today. Using our buildings that otherwise might sit empty six days a week to meet the physical, mental, and emotional needs of children and their families clearly meets Mr. Wesley's expectations.

PRESCHOOL MINISTRY

Weekday preschools are a ministry of the church, and as such should be treated as any other ministry of the church. Make every effort to work with the preschool director and staff to meet the needs of the children served in this ministry. Remember that this may be the only contact that the children have to a faith community. *Guidelines for Weekday Preschool Ministries in United Methodist Congregations* is available through the Ministry with Children website of the General Board of Discipleship. Weekday preschool ministries are diverse, and serve many purposes:

Daycare: A ministry program for infants, toddlers, and pre-elementary children that may begin quite early in the morning and continue late into the evening to accommodate the work schedules of parents. Daycare provides nurture, care, and meals and offers developmentally appropriate activities in a safe atmosphere of love and concern for each child.

Preschool/Nursery School: A half-day to all day ministry program for children up to five years old. Preschool offers developmentally sound curriculum that provides children with experiences and activities that prepare children for kindergarten. Children are taught and nurtured in a safe atmosphere of love and concern for each child.

Kindergarten: A half-day to all day ministry program for children five years of age. Kindergarten offers developmentally sound curriculum that provides children with the readiness skills needed to prepare for entrance into first grade.

Parents' Day/Night Out Program: A half-day, all-day, or evening ministry program of care and activities for children while parents are provided time away.

Play Day: A regular or occasional day for young children to gather with their parents for play. This is a time for parents to interact while their children play safely with them in the church nursery, on the church playground, or at a park.

Care for Special Needs Children: A ministry program for children who are recovering from physical or emotional trauma or abuse, children with disabilities, children for whom English is a second language, or children who have other special needs. This type of ministry program provides a service that may otherwise be unavailable in the community.

AFTER SCHOOL MINISTRY

Before- and After-School Care: A ministry program that provides a safe and enriching atmosphere for elementary school children who otherwise would be without supervision before and after school. Before and After School Care can be extended to a full-time program during the summer or on school holidays to accommodate the needs of working parents. Activities may include educational tutoring, academic enrichment, music lessons, service projects, faith enrichment, and programs addressing special topics.

Small Groups: A ministry for children to share their love of God and neighbor, to fellowship, to learn together, and to engage in Bible study. These groups meet weekly and provide opportunities for children to learn and have fun, while deepening their relationship with God and peers. These groups frequently provide preparation for entry into the church's youth group.

Call Ministry to "Latchkey" Children: A ministry program in which children can call, be called, or communicate via webcam when they are alone at home. This allows children to connect with safe and caring adults.

Non-Church Programs: The church's doors are open to many other programs. The Boy Scouts of America, The Girl Scouts, 4-H, and other groups often use the church facility for meetings and activities. These programs are important in the life of many young people, and The United Methodist Church welcomes them. Children's ministry leaders should make sure that these groups adhere to the policies of the church, including Safe Sanctuaries®.

What Every Child Should Experience

tt he proverb, "Train children in the right way, and when old, they will not stray" shares the importance of training children, but over years, decades, and centuries, we have come to recognize that there are some essentials that children growing up in Christian community should know.

A Scope and Sequence

Based on Scripture, our Wesleyan heritage, our experiences in faith development, and a reasonable look at our call to make disciples of Jesus Christ for the transformation of the world, Children's Ministries of the General Board of Discipleship developed and updates *What Every Child Should Experience: A Guide for Teachers and Leaders in United Methodist Congregations*. This guide outlines a scope and sequence in all of the areas of faith development of children, birth through eleven.

OFFER ALL CHILDREN
- Love and acceptance as children of God
- Clean and safe rooms, equipment, furniture, and toys that fit their size, interests, and abilities
- Trained and caring teachers
- Food, clothing, and shelter as needed
- A welcoming place in worship, fellowship events, and other events where the congregation comes together
- Opportunities for vibrant faith development
- Child care when their parents are involved in church programs

OFFER INFANTS AND TODDLERS:
- Sunday school classes
- Games, music, and creative activities

OFFER PRESCHOOL CHILDREN:
- Sunday school classes
- Music experiences through Sunday school and a children's choir
- Opportunities to be involved in the stewardship program of the church
- Adult friends with whom they feel comfortable
- Mission studies and opportunities for involvement in mission projects
- Encouragement and support when they bring friends with them to church

- Inclusion in corporate worship services of the congregation
- Games, music, and creative activities

OFFER CHILDREN IN THE ELEMENTARY GRADES:
- Sunday school classes and other discipleship learning opportunities
- Opportunities for mission studies that include projects that address justice issues
- Opportunities to be involved in the stewardship program of the church
- Vacation Bible school and special summer programs
- Choir and other music opportunities
- Opportunities to serve in worship through litanies, prayers, Scripture reading, ushering, and serving as acolytes
- Concurrent, appropriate programs when parents are involved in adult church programs
- Encouragement to bring friends to church activities
- Small groups for special concerns such as divorce of parents, death or other significant loss, and serious illness of sibling
- Opportunities for intergenerational relationships

OFFER PARENTS OF CHILDREN:
- Opportunities for continuing and vibrant faith development
- Parenting classes
- Food, clothing, shelter as needed
- Assurance of a safe place for their children
- Small groups for special concerns such as loss of a child or spouse, child abuse, substance abuse, or divorce
- Support from the pastor, professional educator, and church staff
- Opportunities to learn about baptism, Communion, and worship
- Information on what their children are studying
- Resources to support them as their child's first teacher
- Information on community issues that affects children and the role of the church in the community

Finding Support and Guidance

One of the blessings of The United Methodist Church is connection. No one is alone in ministry thanks to the structure of the Church. Support and guidance can be found in many places. A contact person who works with the annual conference will support your ministry by offering specific training and directing you to helpful resources. The General Board of Discipleship will support your ministry by developing resources, providing training for teachers and leaders, researching best practices, and helping you connect to the people and resources that you need in your church setting. The General

Board of Higher Education and Ministry offers certification in children's ministry for those who are called into this ministry. The General Board of Global Ministries responds to the needs of the most vulnerable of society—our children. The General Board of Church and Society advocates for the rights of children. All of these groups work to support the children's ministries in the local church as you make disciples of Jesus Christ for the transformation of the world.

May the grace of our Lord Jesus Christ be with your spirit, Brothers and Sisters. Amen.

Resources

Items marked as (GBOD) are available at www.gbod.org/children unless another GBOD location is specified.

BASIC UNDERSTANDING OF MINISTRY WITH CHILDREN

Baptism: Understanding God's Gift, by Edward and Sara Webb Phillips (GBOD). A guide for parents and guardians preparing to present their children for baptism and for those who seek a deeper knowledge of baptism.

Child Care and the Church (GBOD). Official document of The United Methodist Church outlining responsibilities in initiating, encouraging, and participating in the highest quality of child care.

The Children's Minister, by Rita B. Hays (Nashville: Discipleship Resources, 2008. ISBN 978-088177-527-3). Helps those in ministry with children connect with the lives and pastoral needs of children.

The Most Important Space in the Church, by Rita B. Hays (Nashville: Discipleship Resources, 2009. ISBN 978-0-88177-568-6). Emphasizes that evangelism and spiritual formation begin in the nursery.

Real Kids, Real Faith—Practices for Nurturing Children's Spiritual Lives, by Karen Marie Yust (San Francisco: Jossey Bass, 2004. ISBN 978-0-78796-4078). Insight and helpful tips for nurturing children's spiritual and religious formation.

Training Model in Children's Ministry (GBOD or your annual conference office). Web-based training that covers the basics of the importance of ministry with children, including developmental, safety, and theological issues.

United Methodist Publishing House Curriculum Comparison Chart (GBOD). Includes curriculum approved by the Curriculum Resources Committee for use in the Christian education ministry.

WEEKDAY MINISTRIES

Afterschool Alliance (www.afterschoolalliance.org). Works to ensure that all youth have access to affordable, quality afterschool programs.

Developmentally Appropriate Practice in Early Childhood Programs Guidelines for Weekday Preschools in United Methodist Churches, by Gail

Callis, Lynne Paredes, and Melanie C. Gordon (GBOD). Lays out the basic guidelines for administrating an effective weekday preschool ministry in United Methodist churches.

Legal Manual of the UMC (Contact www.gcfa.org in the Resources tab). A resource from the General Council on Finance and Administration's responsibility to protect the legal interests of the denomination.

Scouting Ministry (Available through the United Methodist Men). Resources and support for how to use civic youth-serving agencies as an outreach ministry within their community (www.gcumm.org).

Serving Children from Birth Through Age 8 (3d ed.), by Carol Copple and Sue Bredekamp (Available through The National Association for the Education of Young Children www.naeyc.org. ISBN: 9781928896647). Assists in identifying and implementing developmentally appropriate experiences and opportunities for young children.

United Methodist Association of Preschools-Florida (Contact www.umapfl.com). Information and support in the area of accreditation for weekday preschool ministry nationally.

SAFE SANCTUARIES®: KEEPING CHILDREN SAFE
Safe Sanctuaries—Reducing the Risk of Abuse in the Church for Children and Youth, by Joy Melton (Nashville: Discipleship Resources, 2008. ISBN: 978-0-88177-543-3). Practical guidance is provided in developing and implementing a substantive, holistic action plan of abuse prevention.

Safe Sanctuaries® (GBOD). An online guide to contacts, resources, laws, and forms that help congregations make a safe place for children.

FORMATIONAL STUDIES AND LESSONS FOR CHILDREN
Children and Worship (GBOD). Resources that support including children in worship and the life of the congregation.

Godly Play (Contact www.godlyplayfoundation.org/newsite/Main.php). Teaches children as young as three the art of using religious language.

The Way of the Child (Contact http://bookstore.upperroom.org/). A formative study for children ages six through eleven.

NEWSLETTERS AND RESOURCE INFORMATION

"inFORMATION" Memos (GBOD). Addresses children's issues in quick and easy free downloads for leaders in ministry with children.

iTeach (www.gbod.org/education). Free monthly e-newsletter providing insights and thought-provoking observations.

Ministry with Children eNewsletter (GBOD). Addresses topics of concern for those engaged in ministry for children. Also available in PDF form.

UM Ministry with Children Blog (GBOD). Support, resources, and connections for those engaged in ministry for children, birth to eleven.

FAITH DEVELOPMENT AND FORMATION

Development through the Lifespan Chart (GBOD). Outlines twelve different stages of development throughout the lifespan.

What Every Child Should Experience: A Guide for Leaders and Teachers in United Methodist Congregations, by Melanie C. Gordon (GBOD). Free, comprehensive scope and sequence supports teachers and leaders in addressing the scriptural, developmental, and formational needs of children.

TRAINING OPPORTUNITIES

General Board of Discipleship of The United Methodist Church (GBOD). Resources, training, and support for leaders engaged in ministry with children.

UM Conference on Children's Ministries (GBOD). National conference [formerly FOCUS] that offers workshops, networking, training, and certification classes for those engaged in ministry with children. Occurs biannually with web-based training during opposite years.

Web-Based Training (GBOD). Connects leaders and teachers engaged in ministry with children the opportunity to learn new skills and address timely issues with leaders in specific areas that concern faith formation of children.

RESOURCE AGENCIES AND ORGANIZATIONS

Children's Defense Fund (Contact www.childrensdefense.org). Non-profit agency that advocates for the rights of children in the United States, sponsoring Freedom Schools for Youth and Children's Sabbath for Children.

Christian Educators Fellowship (Contact www.cefumc.org). Professional affiliate organization for those leading Christian Education ministries in congregations; national organization with chapters in annual conferences.

National Association for the Education of Young Children (Contact www.neayc.org). Professional organization that promotes excellence in early childhood education and provides resources and training.

MISSION OPPORTUNITIES FOR CHILDREN

Heifer International (www.heifer.org). Works with communities to end hunger and poverty and care for the earth by giving families a hand-up.

The United Methodist Children's Fund for Christian Mission (GBOD). Teaches children about mission work and allows them to contribute to projects that help other children.

United Methodist Committee on Relief (www.gbgm-umc.org/umcor). Provides supply kits for assistance during times of crisis.

UNICEF (Contact www.unicef.org). Helps build a world where the rights of every child are realized.

ZOE Ministry (www.zoeministry.org). Gives orphans the resources and support they need to break the cycle of poverty and dependency forever.

MAGAZINES FOR CHILDREN AND FAMILIES

The Little Christian Magazine (Available through the Evangelical Lutheran Church of America). Contains faith-based stories meant to be read by or with young children.

Pockets Magazine (www.upperrroom.org/bookstore). Devotional magazine that helps children ages six through eleven learn more about God.

GENERAL CHURCH RESOURCES

The Book of Discipline of The United Methodist Church, 2012 (Contact www.Cokesbury.com).

Guidelines for Leading Your Congregation 2013–2016 (Contact www.Cokesbury.com).

United Methodist Program Calendar 2012 (Contact www.Cokesbury.com).